HEADRUSH
SKULL
TATTOO AND DOODLES PATTERNS

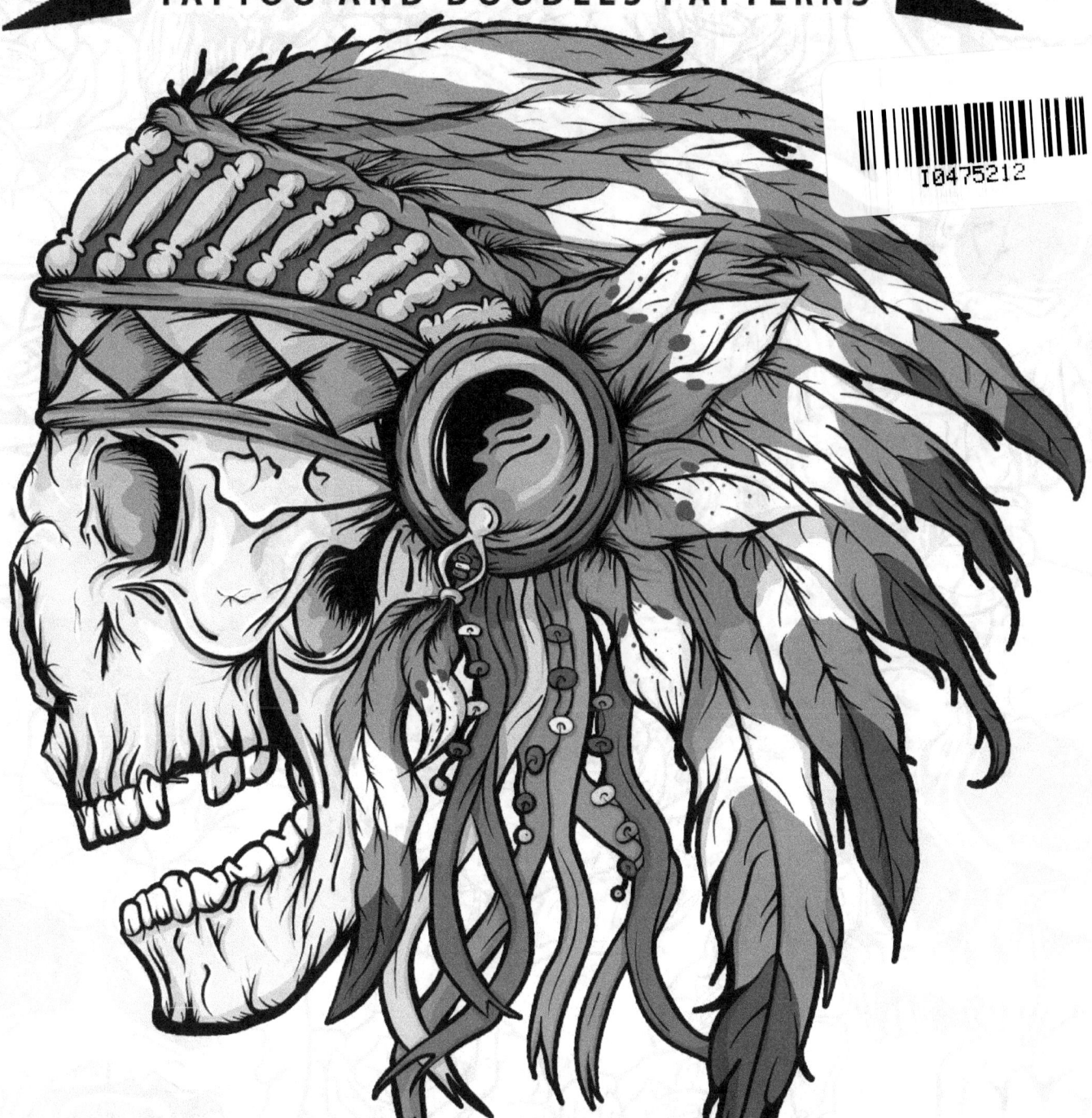

I0475212

COLORING BOOK FOR ADULTS

COLOR TEST PAGE

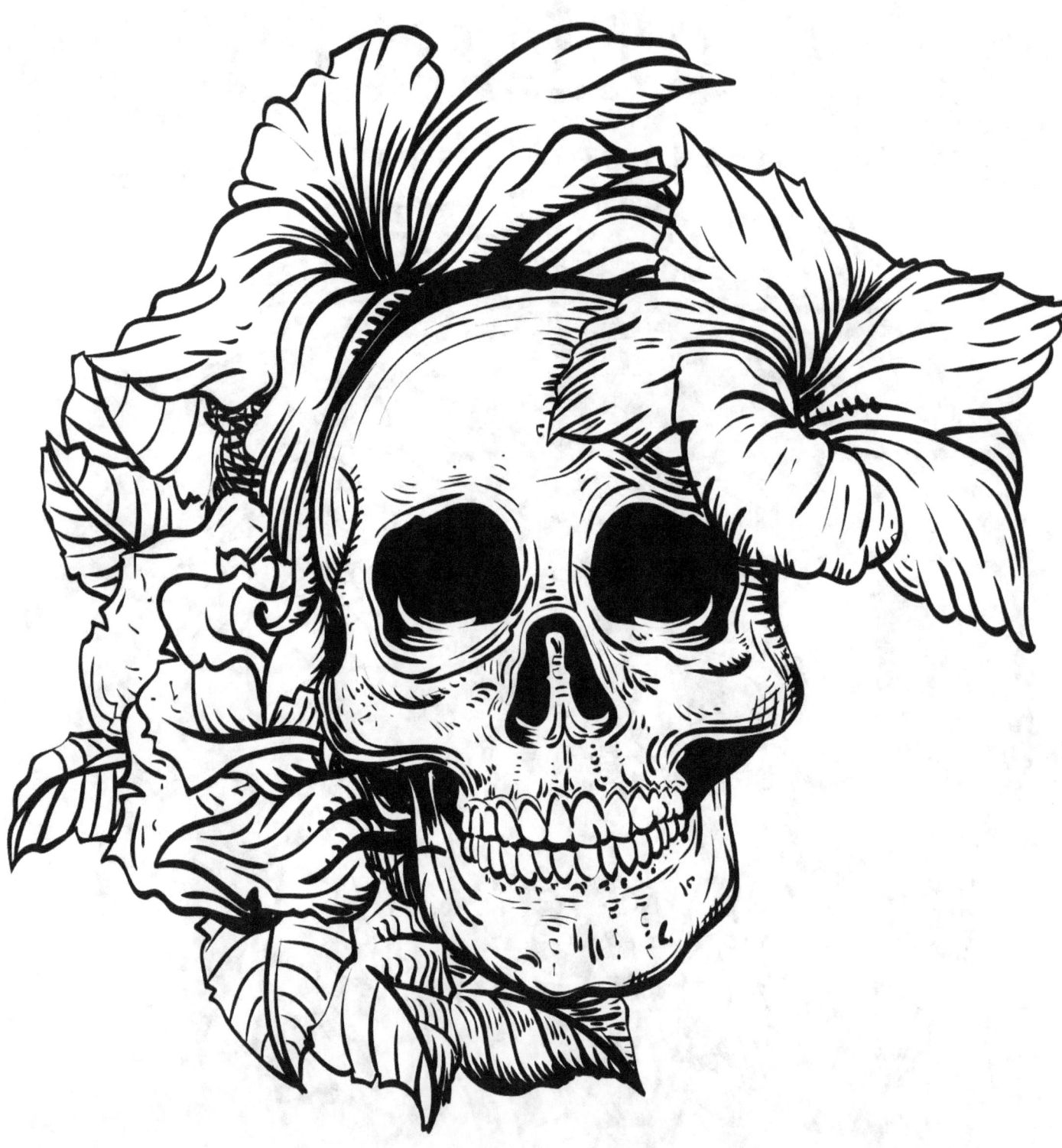

COLOR TEST PAGE

TEST YOUR COLOR

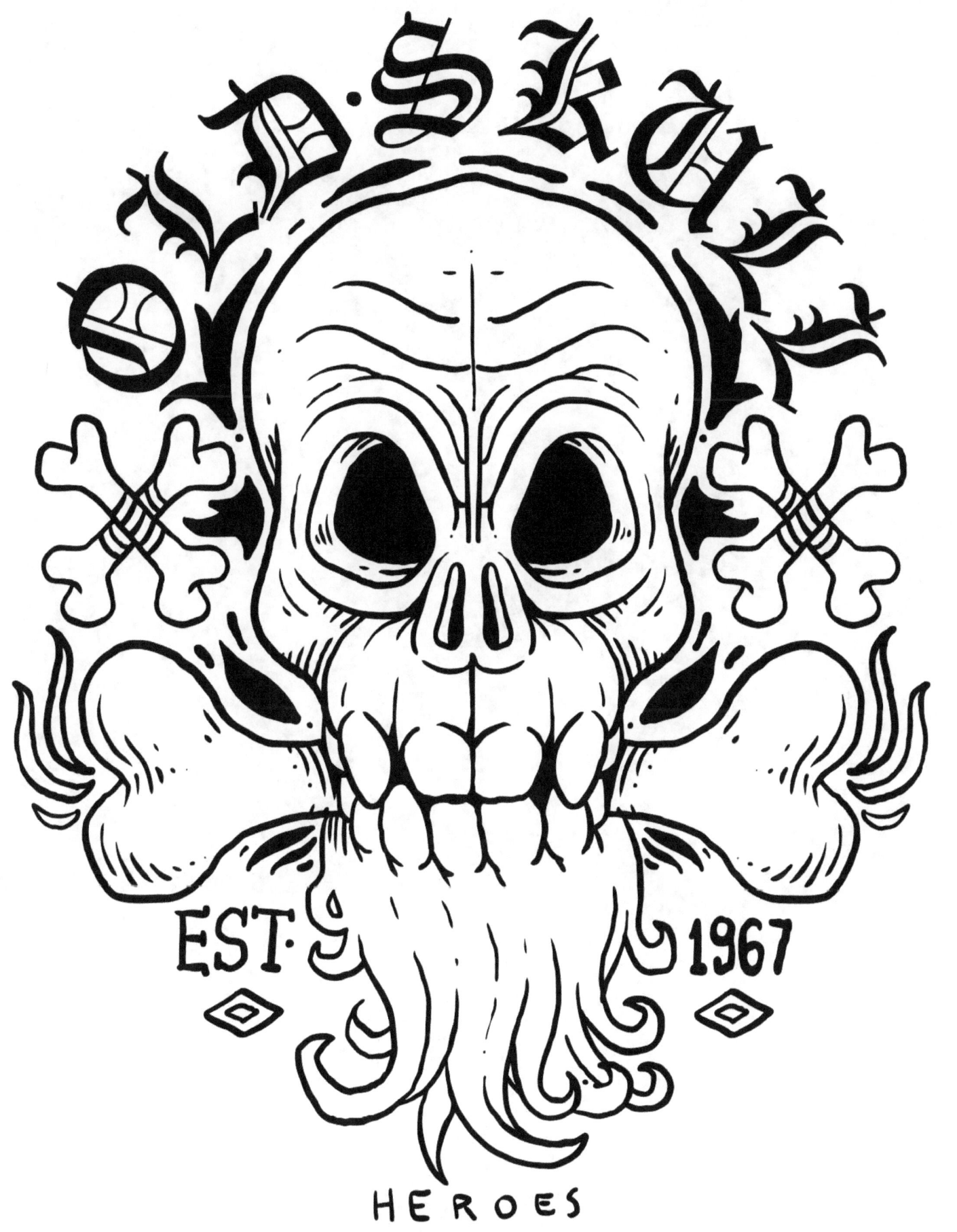

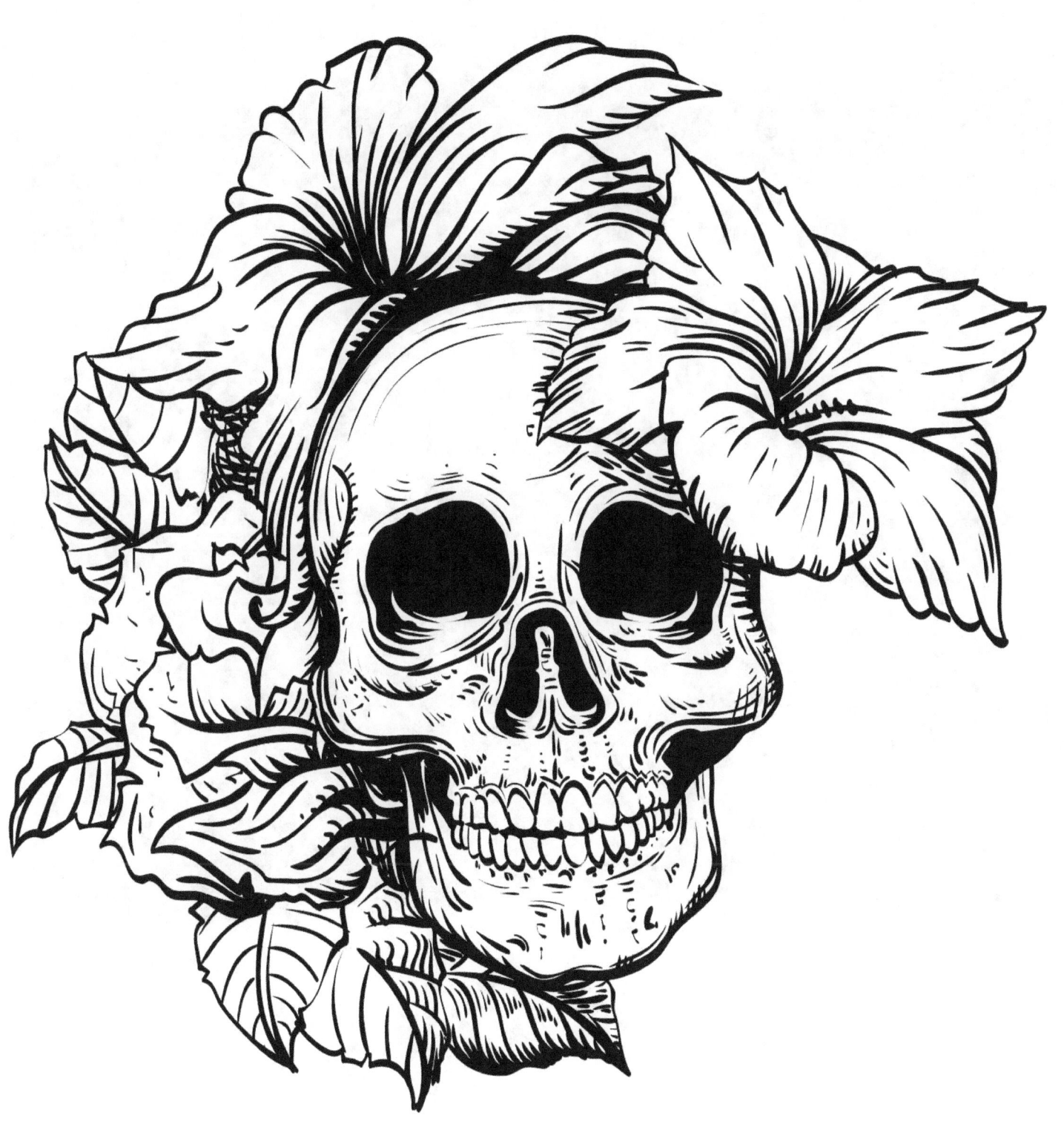

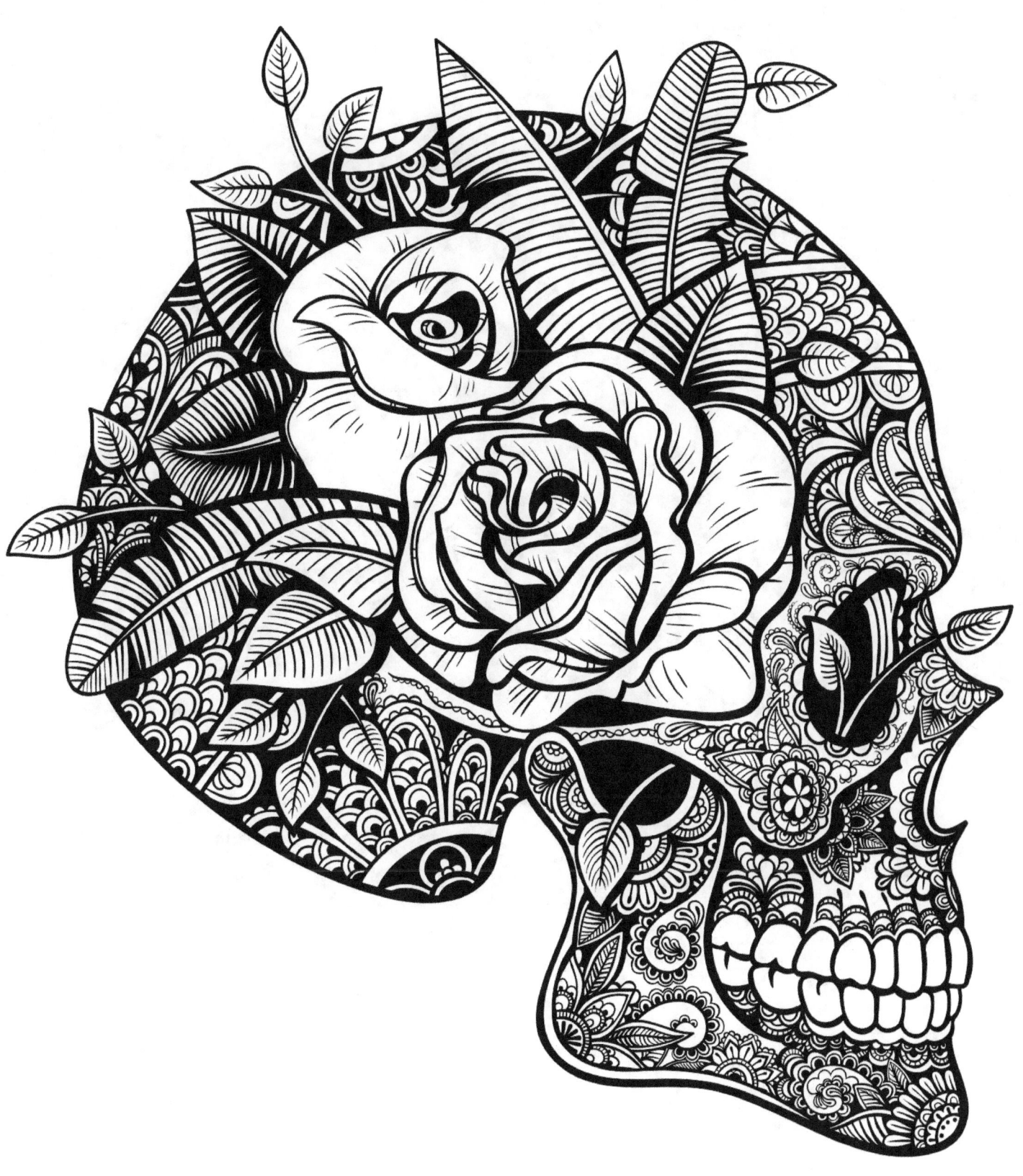

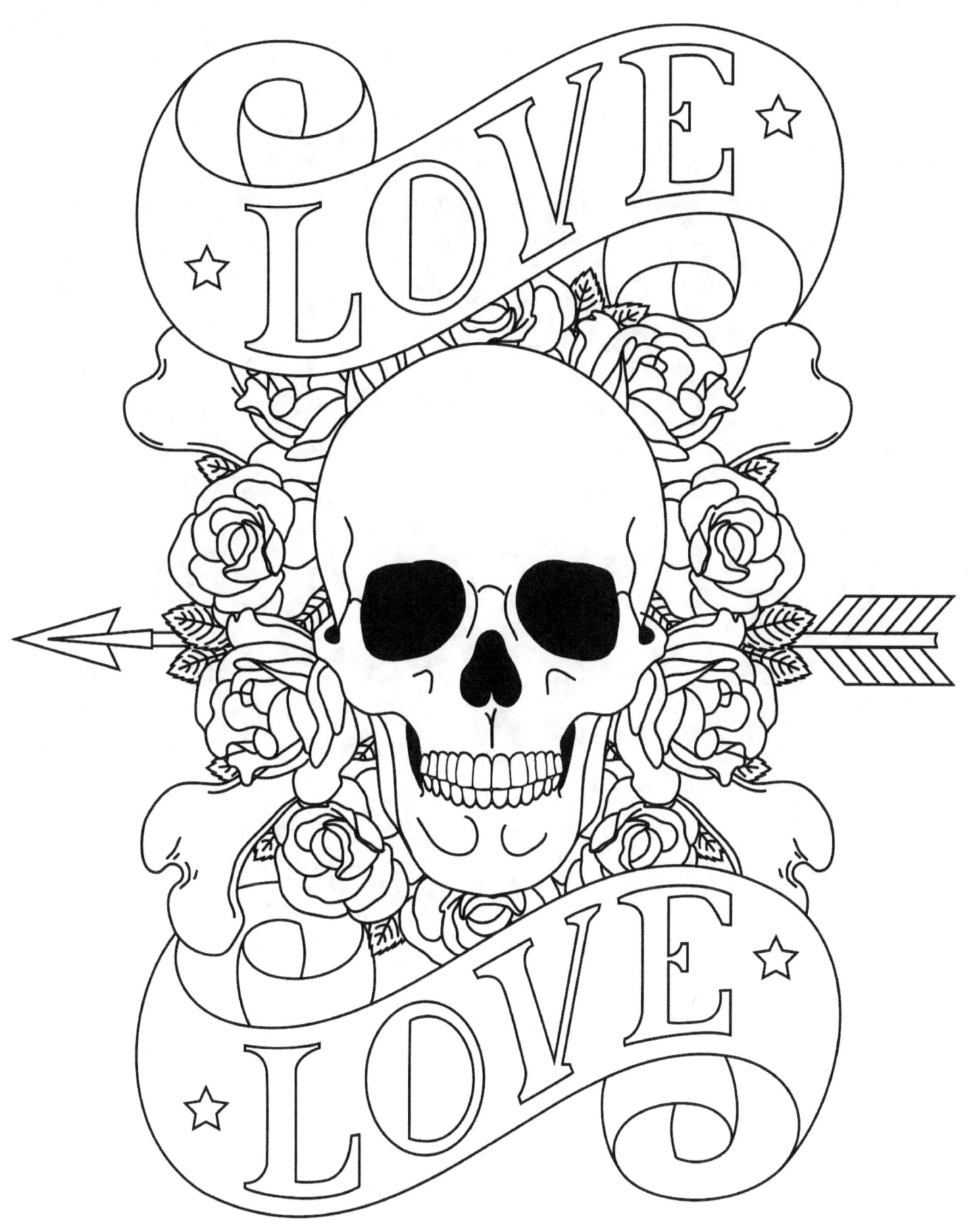

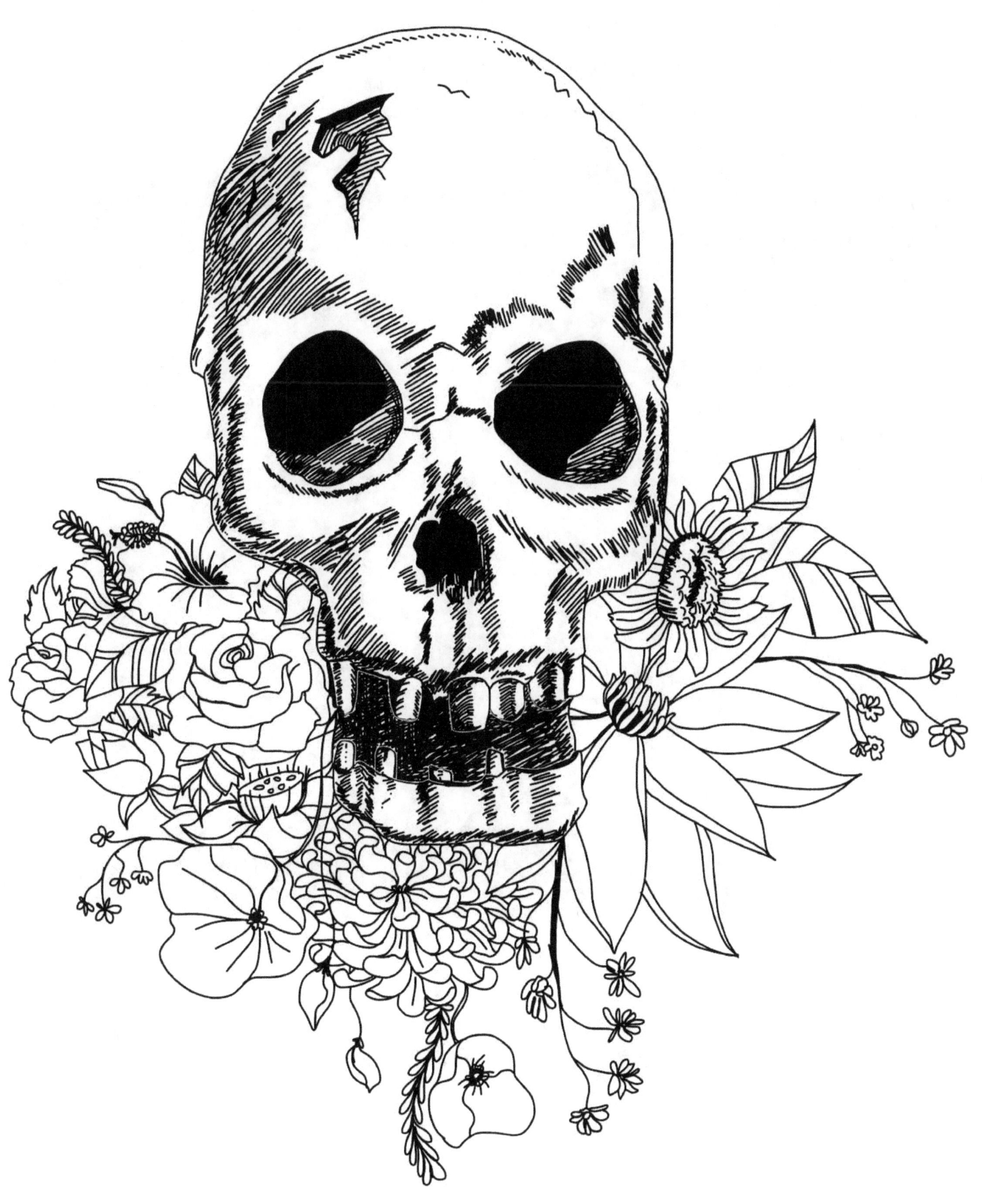

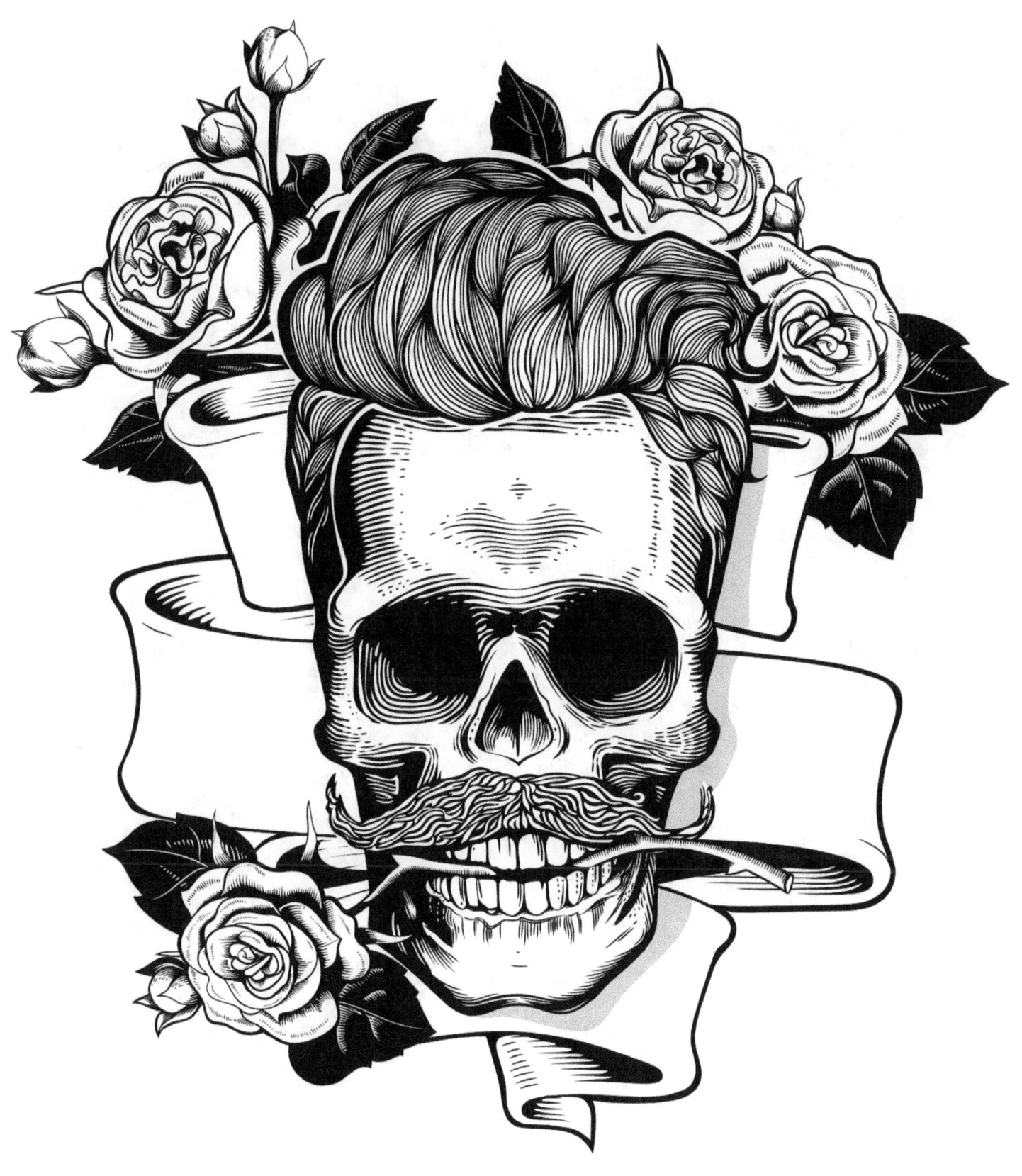

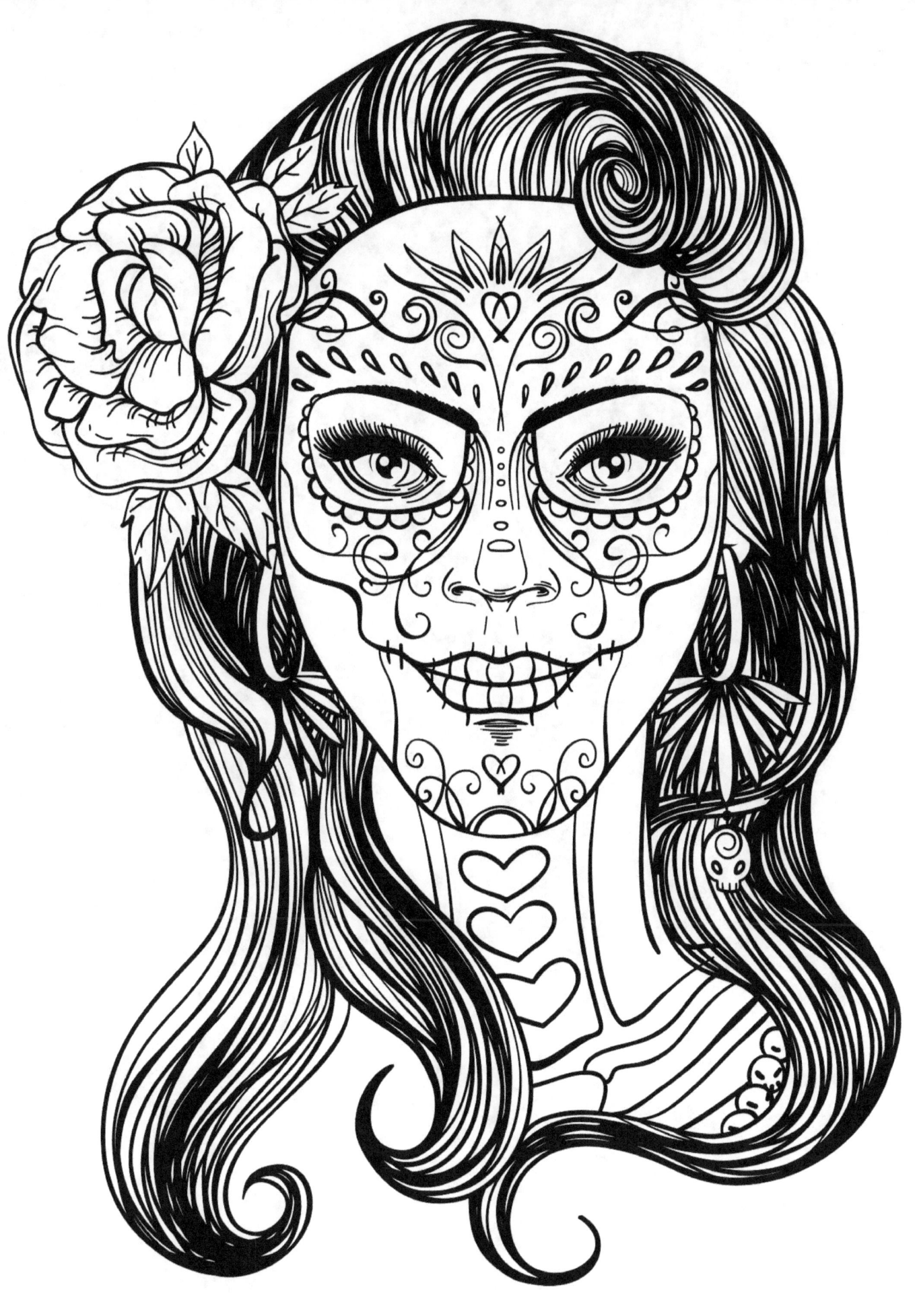

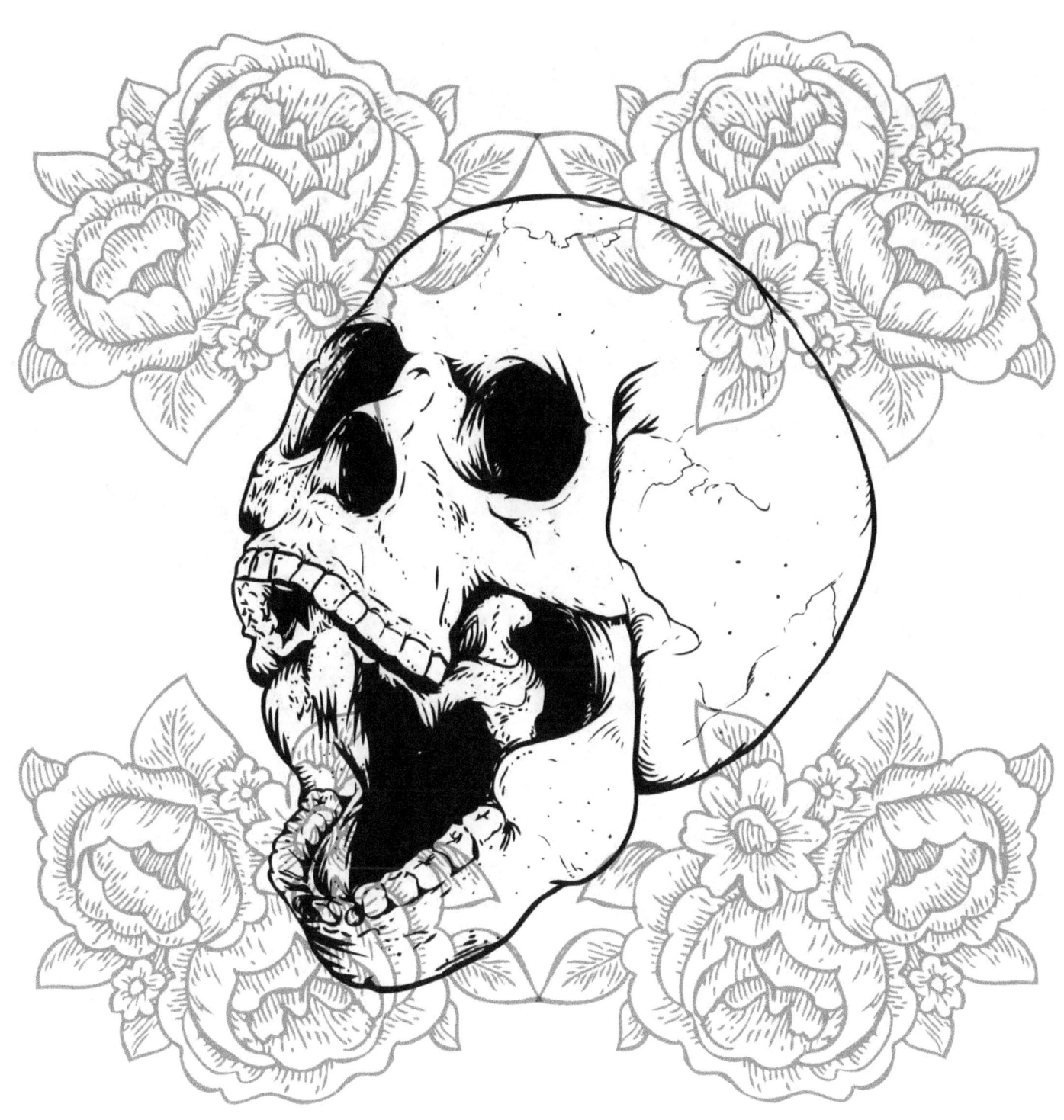

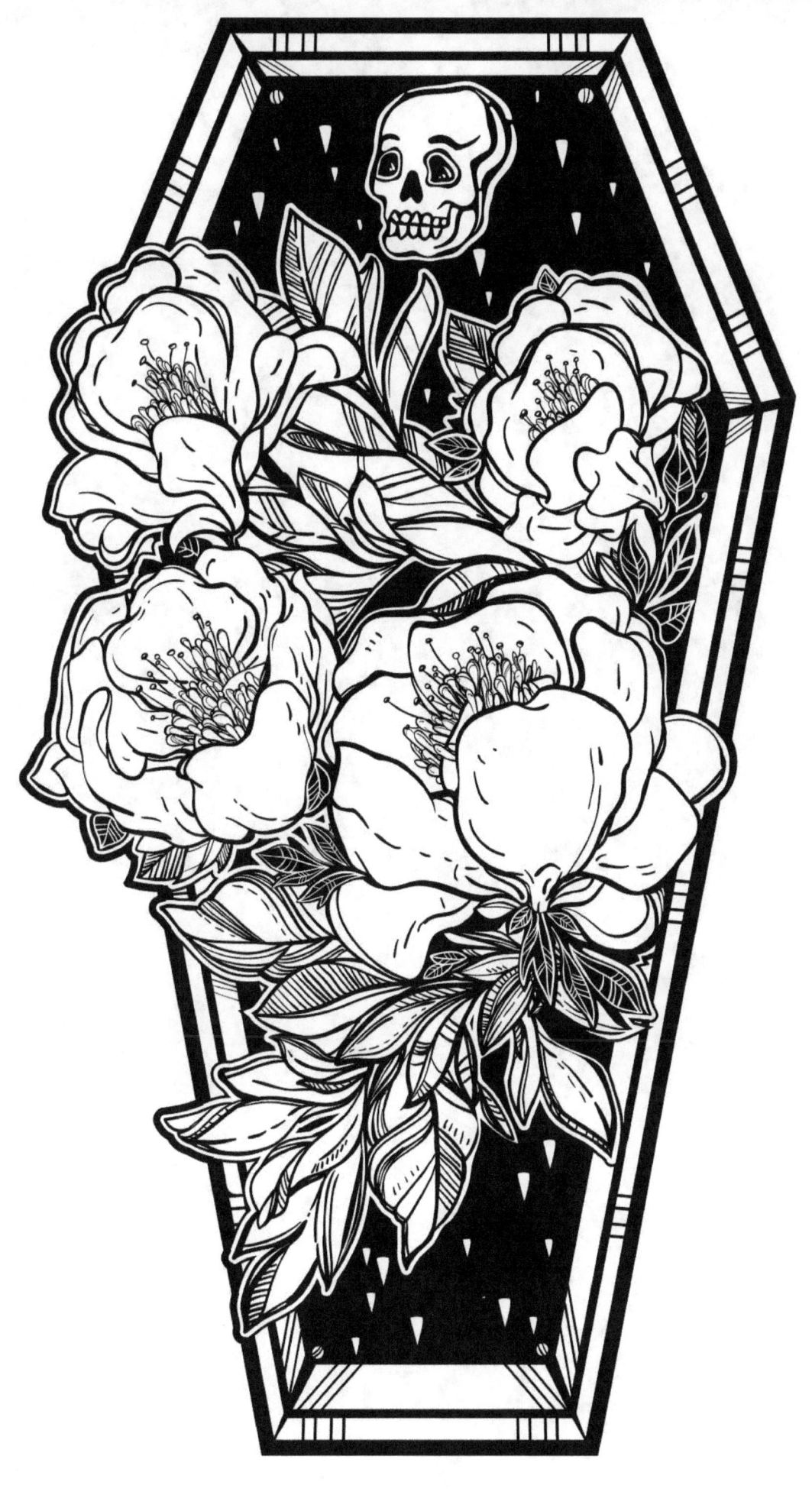

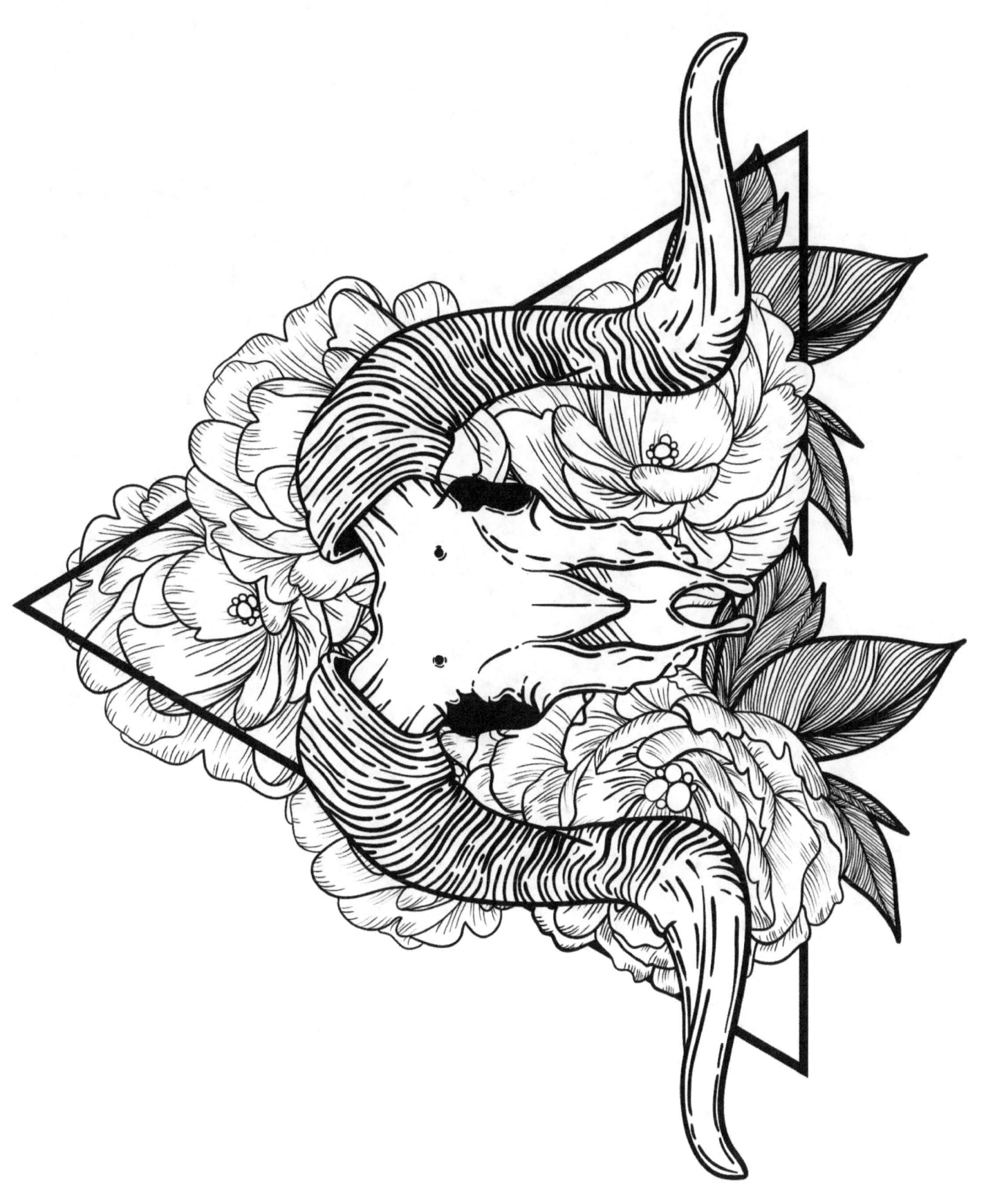

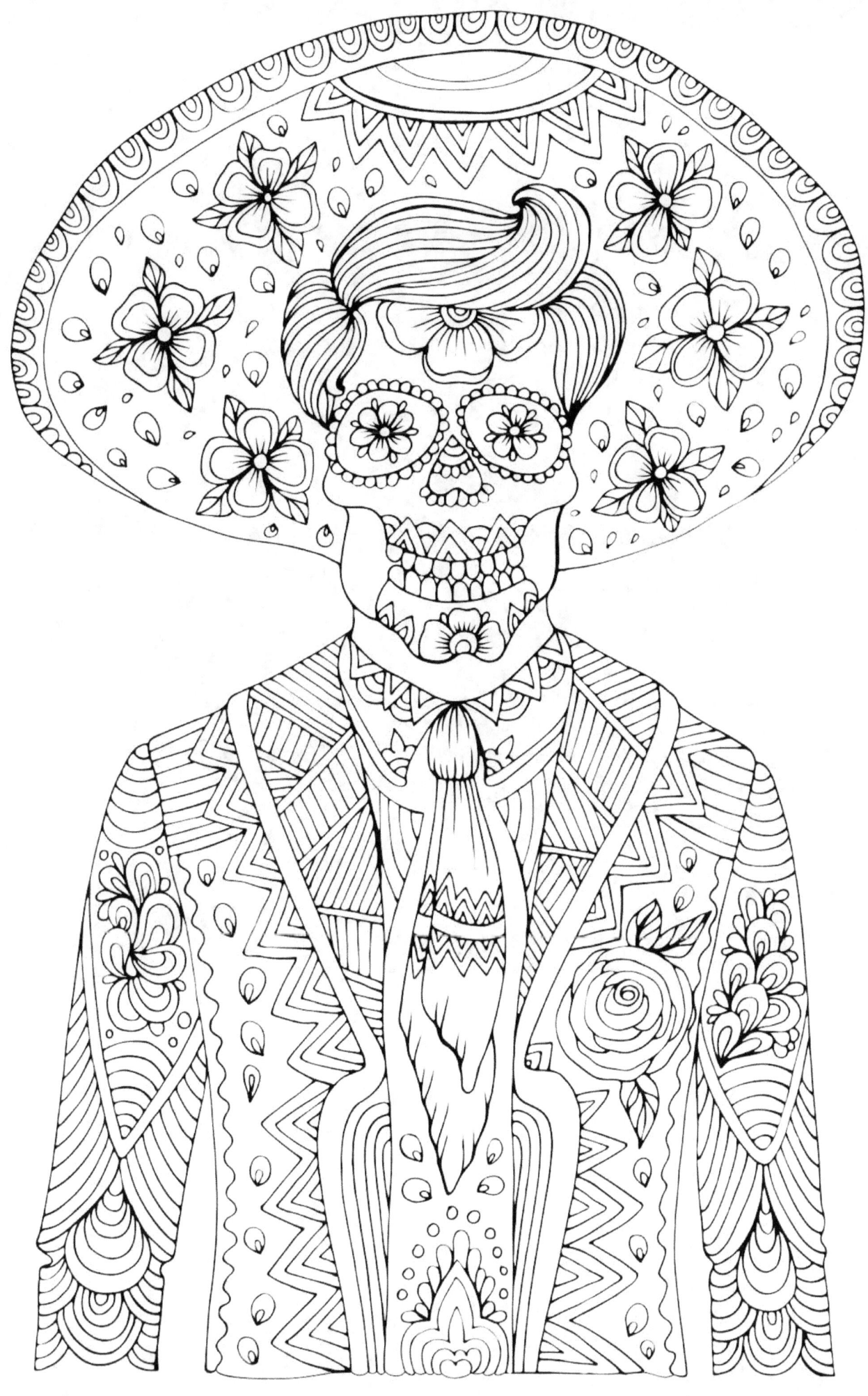

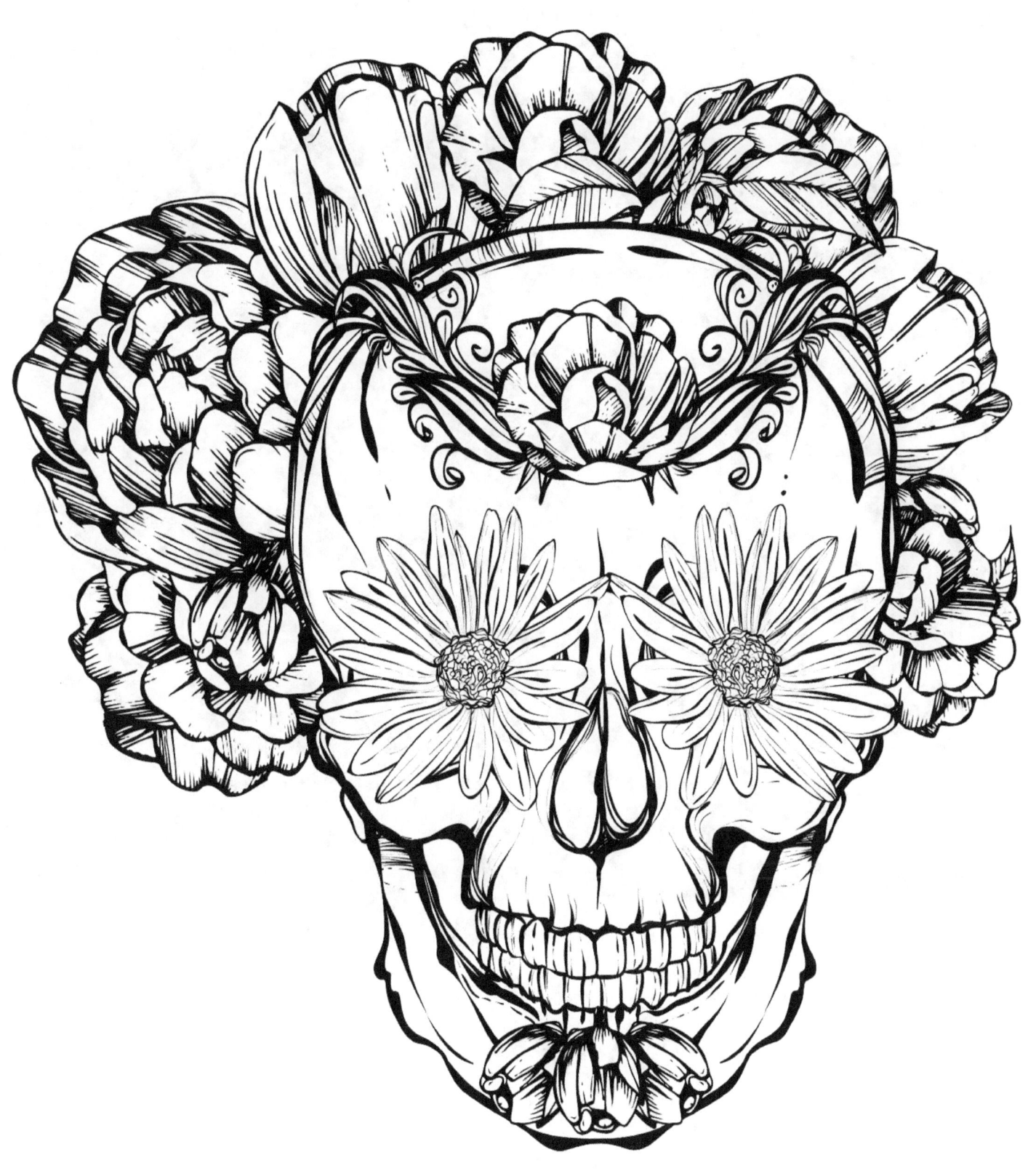

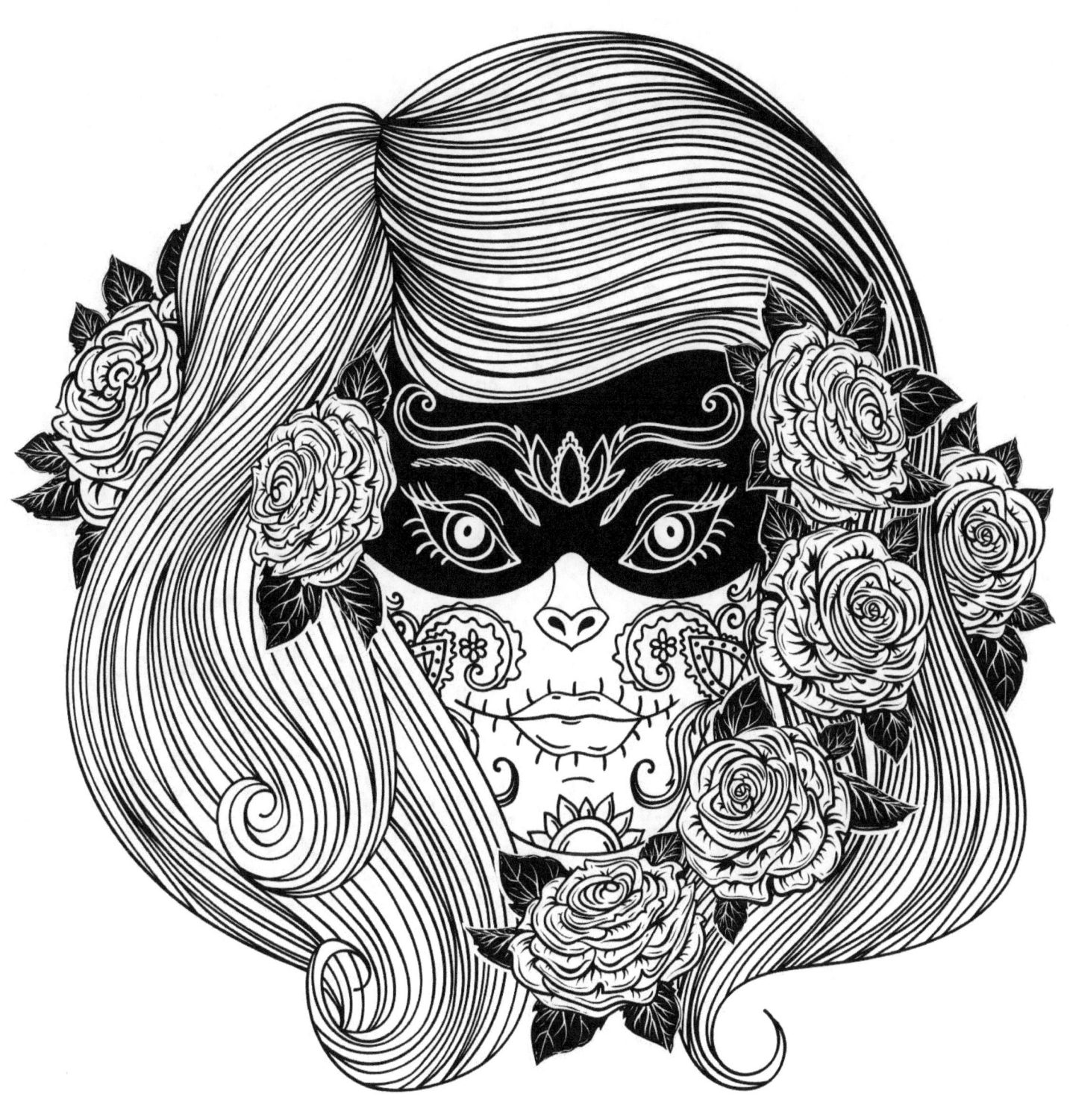

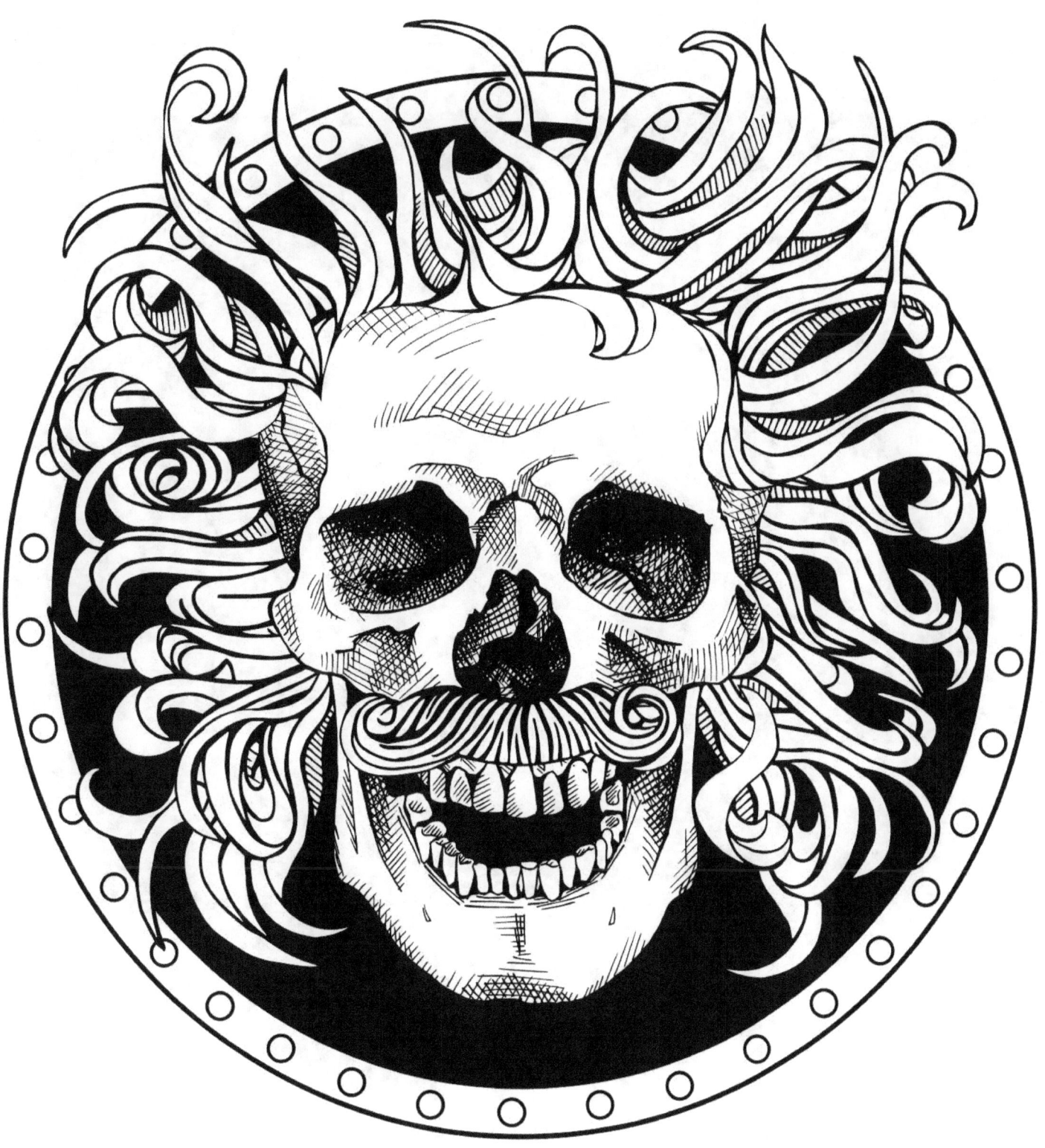

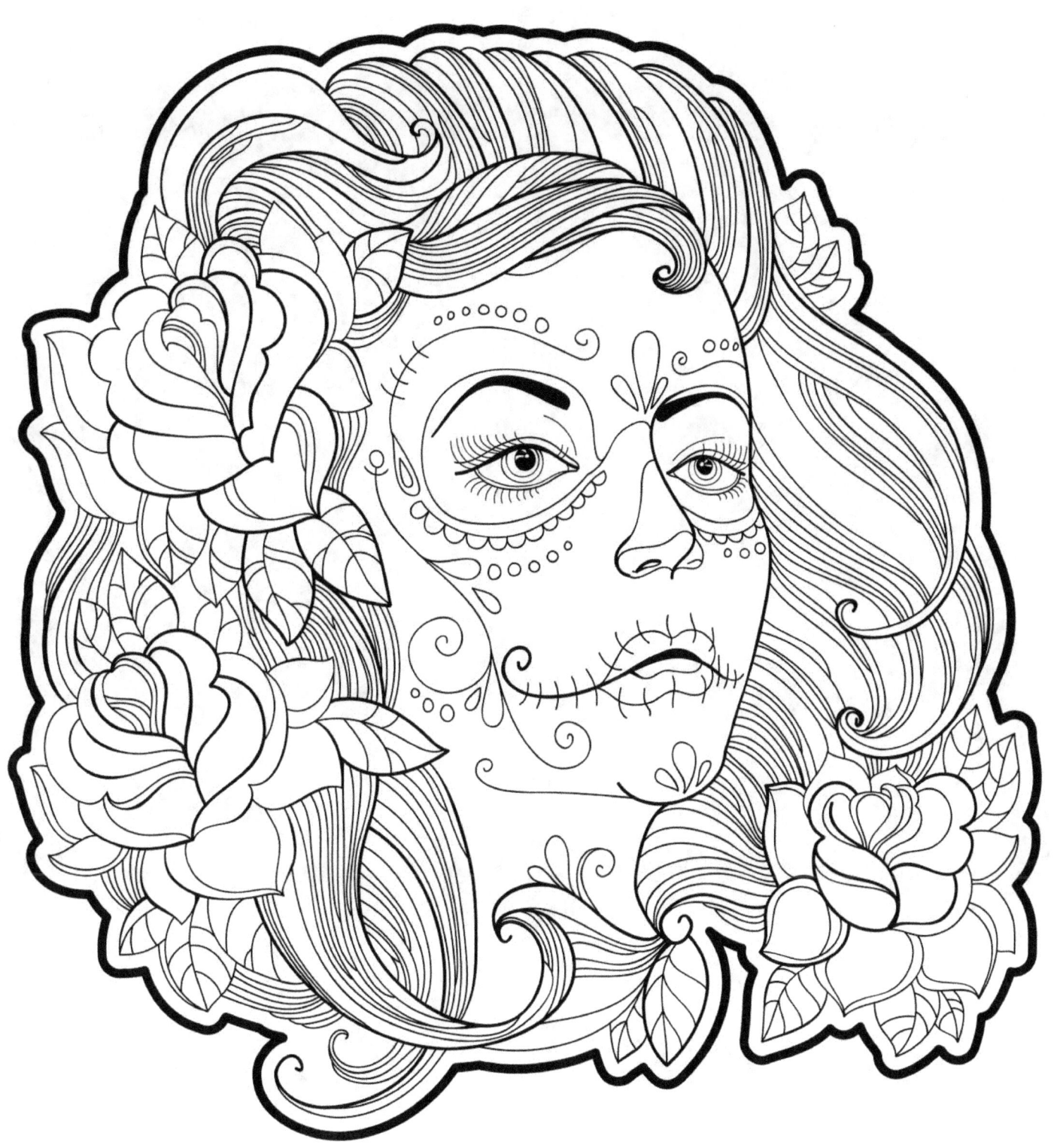

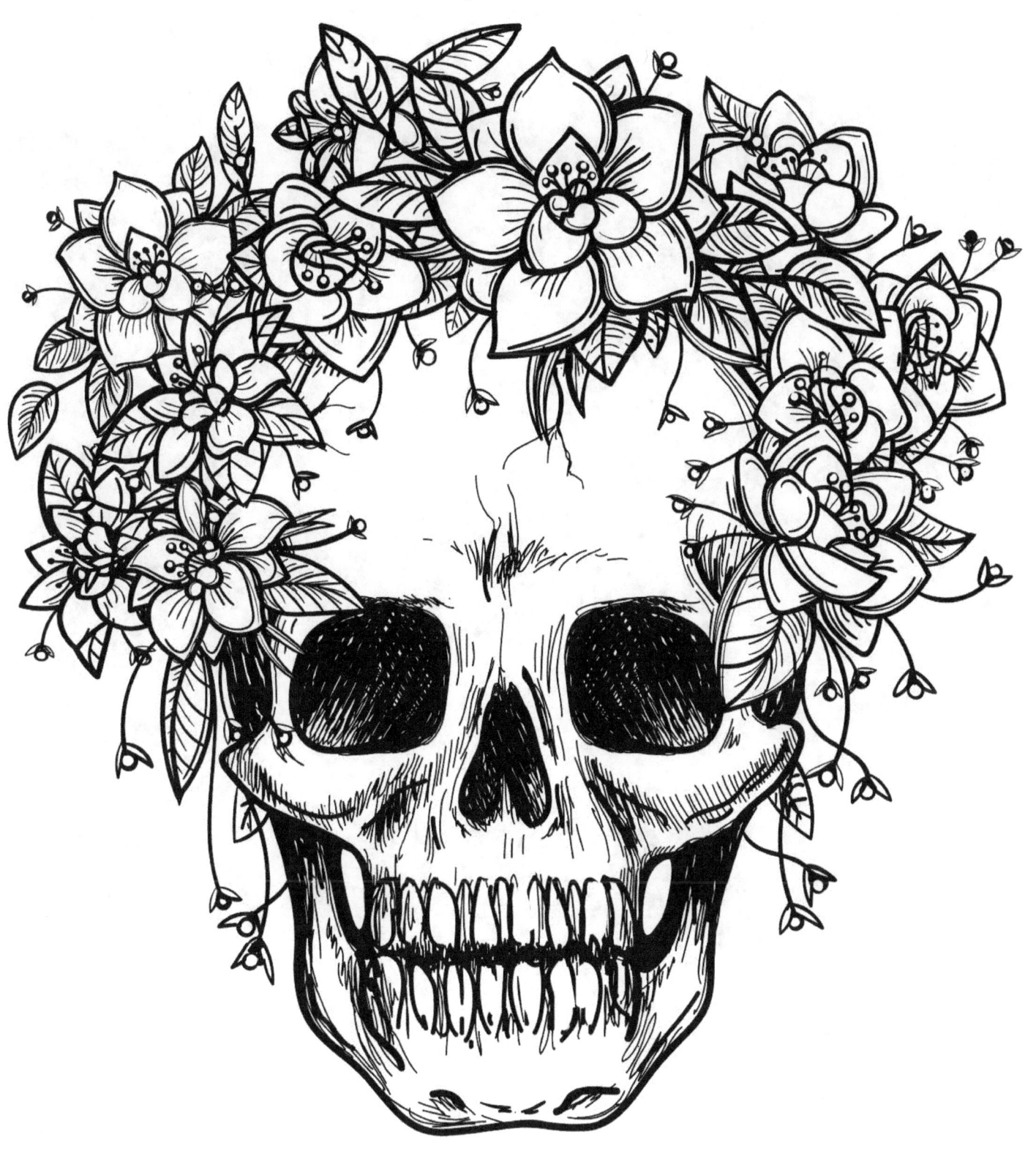

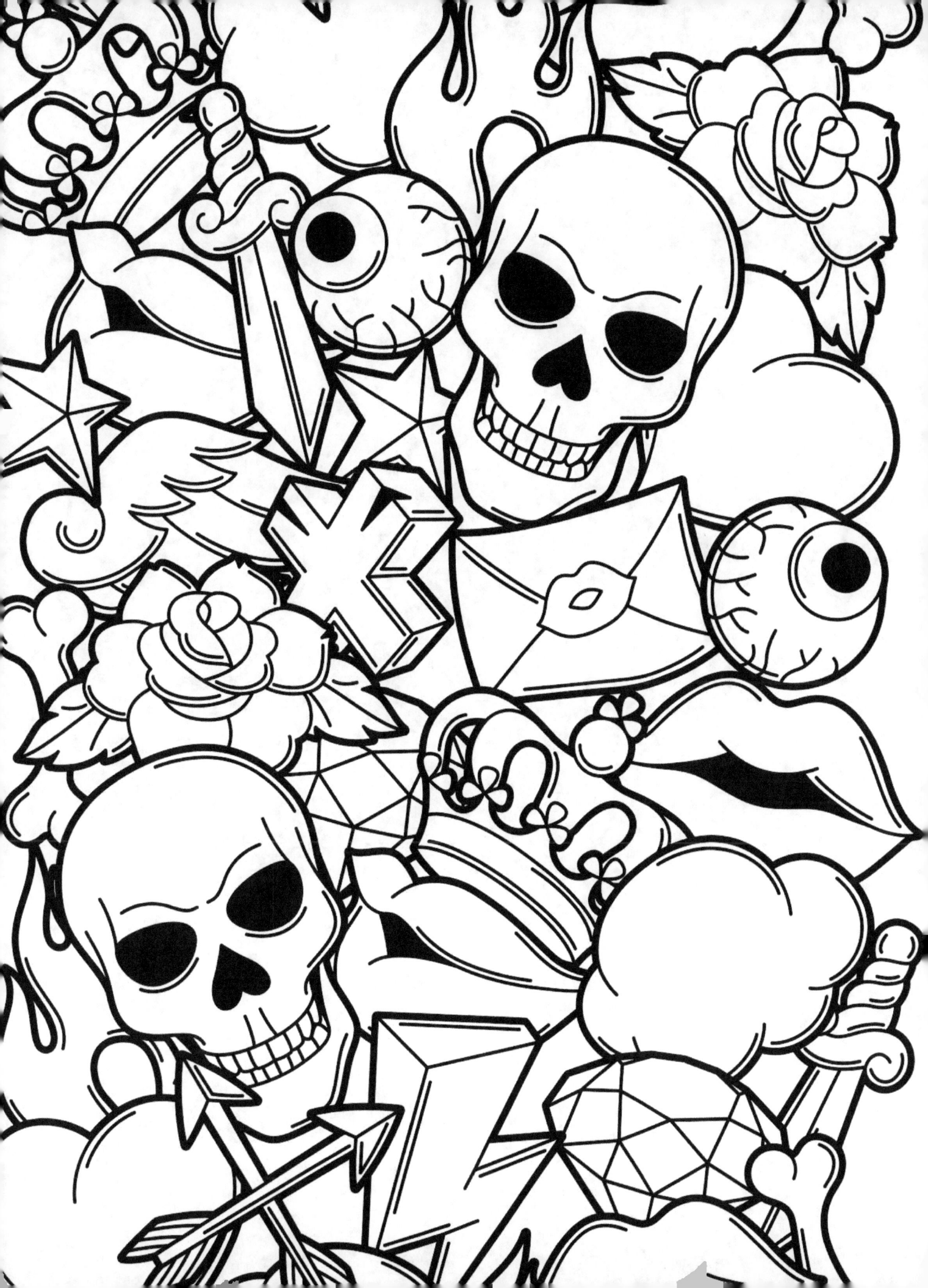

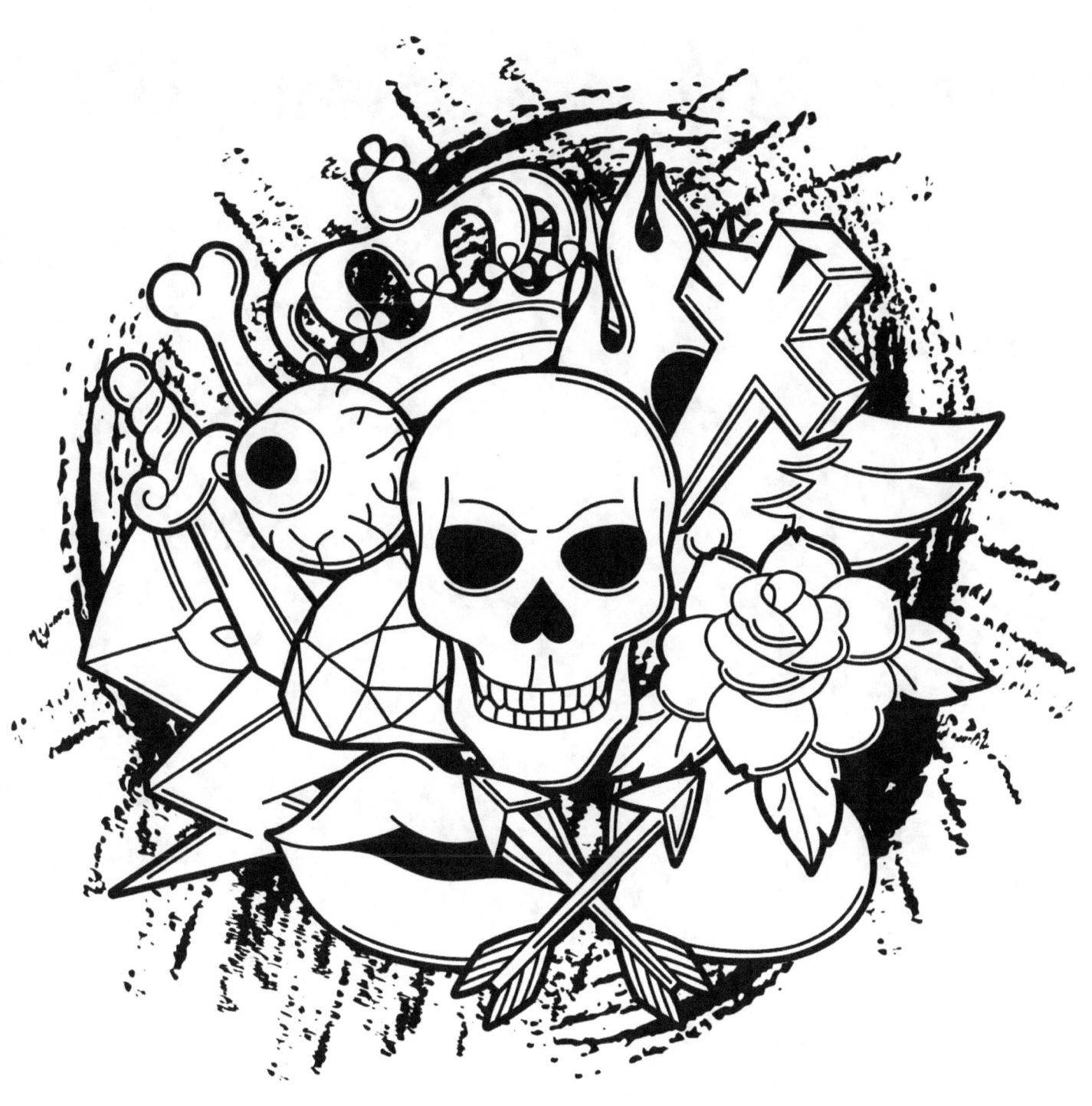

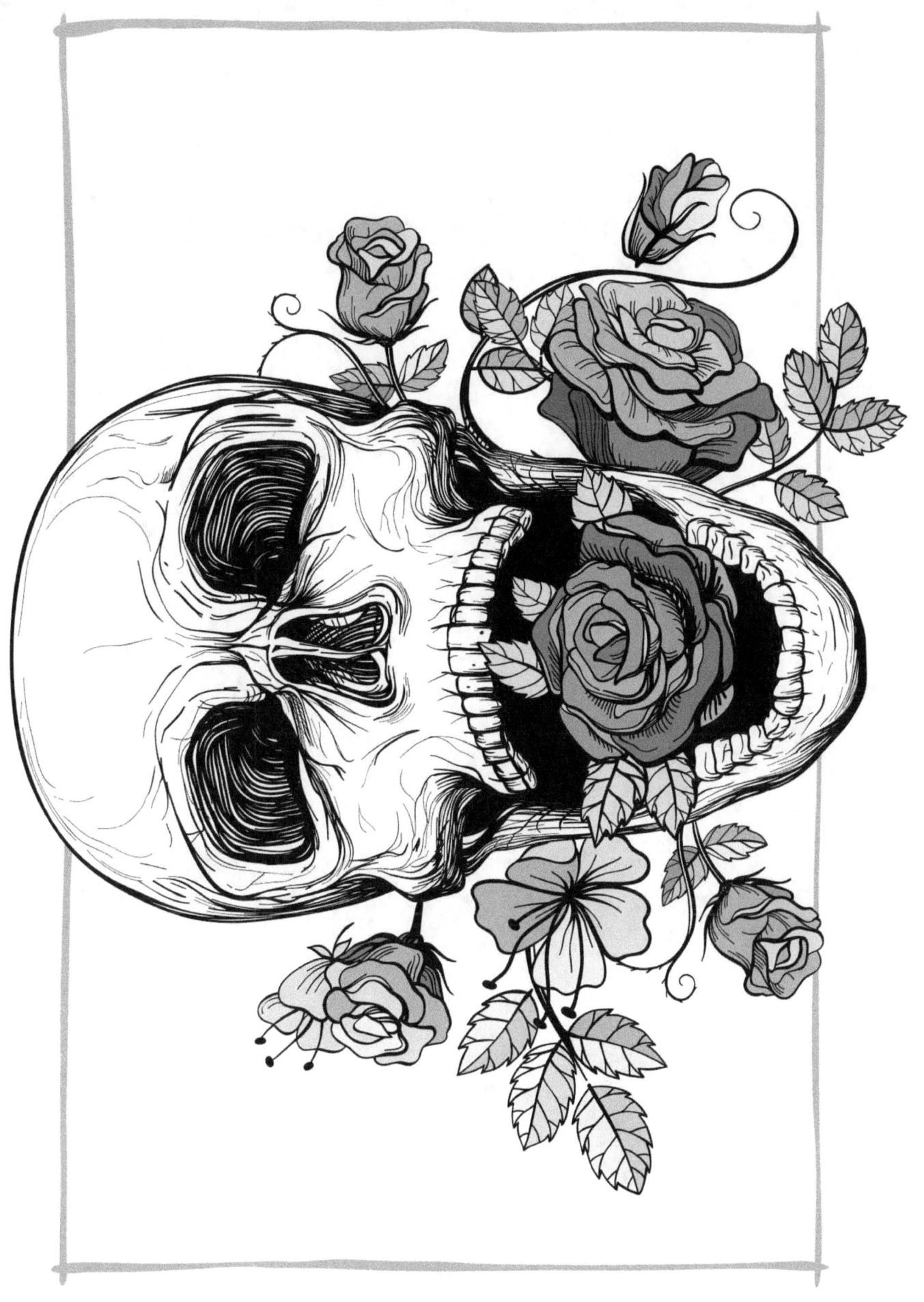

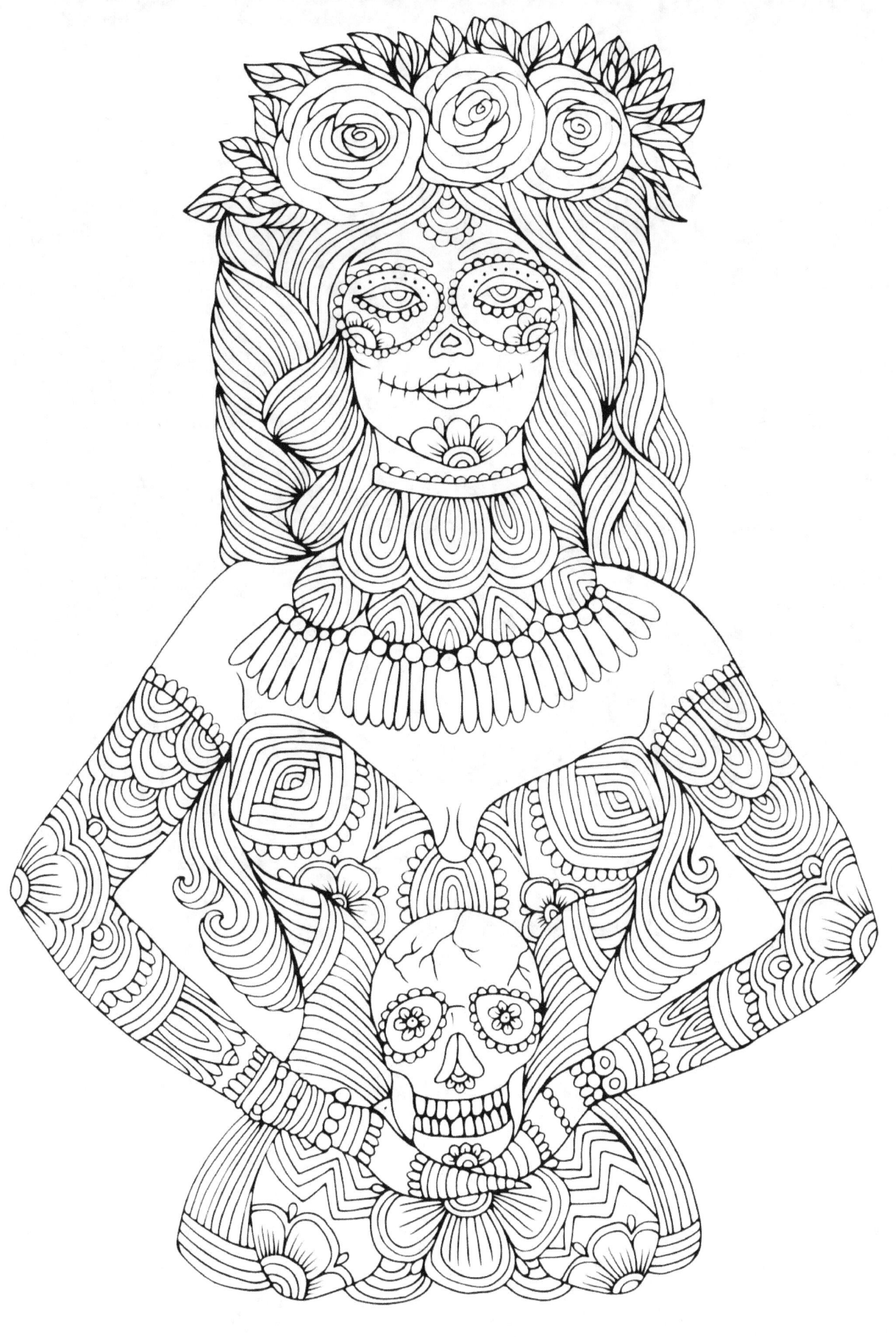

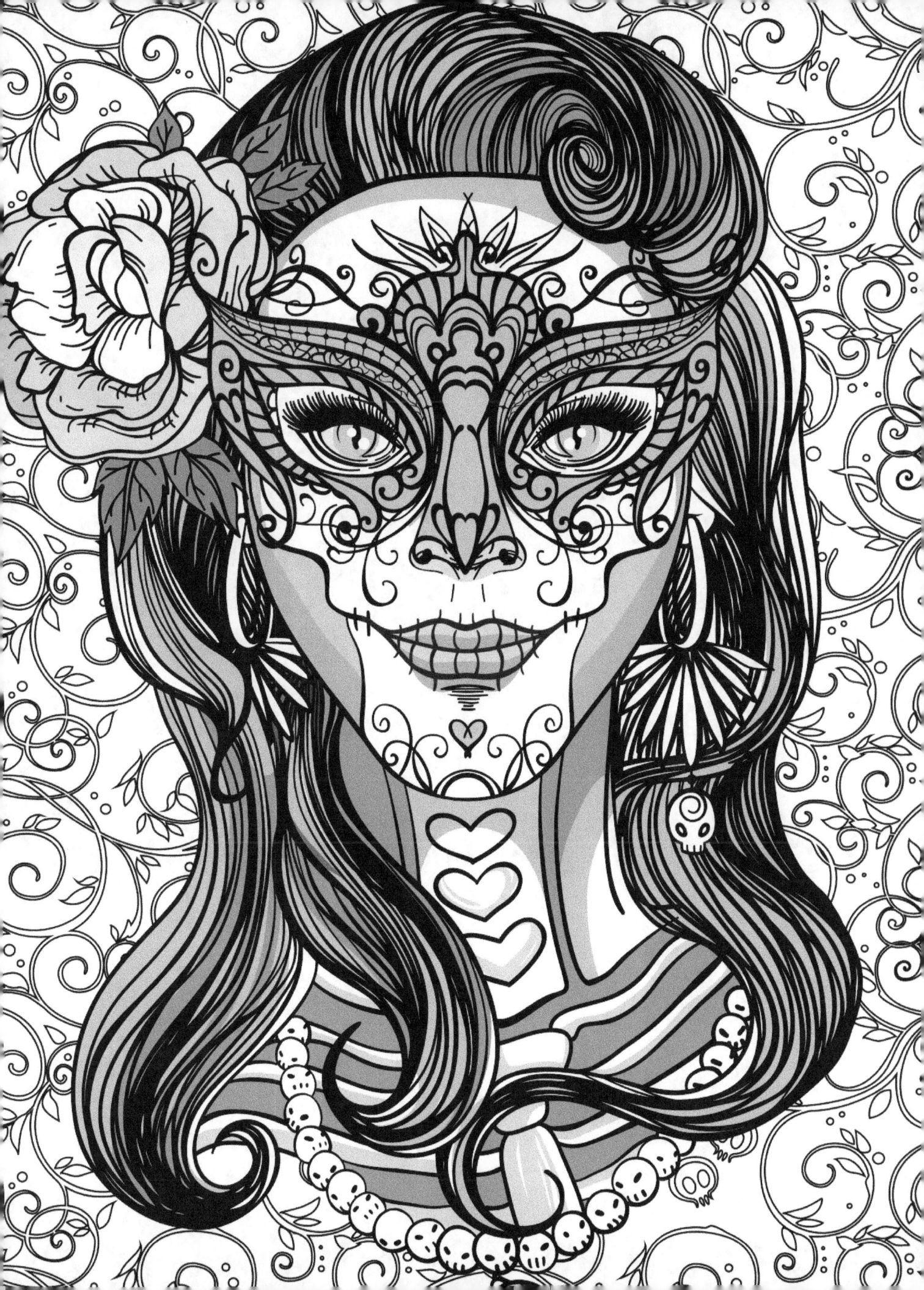

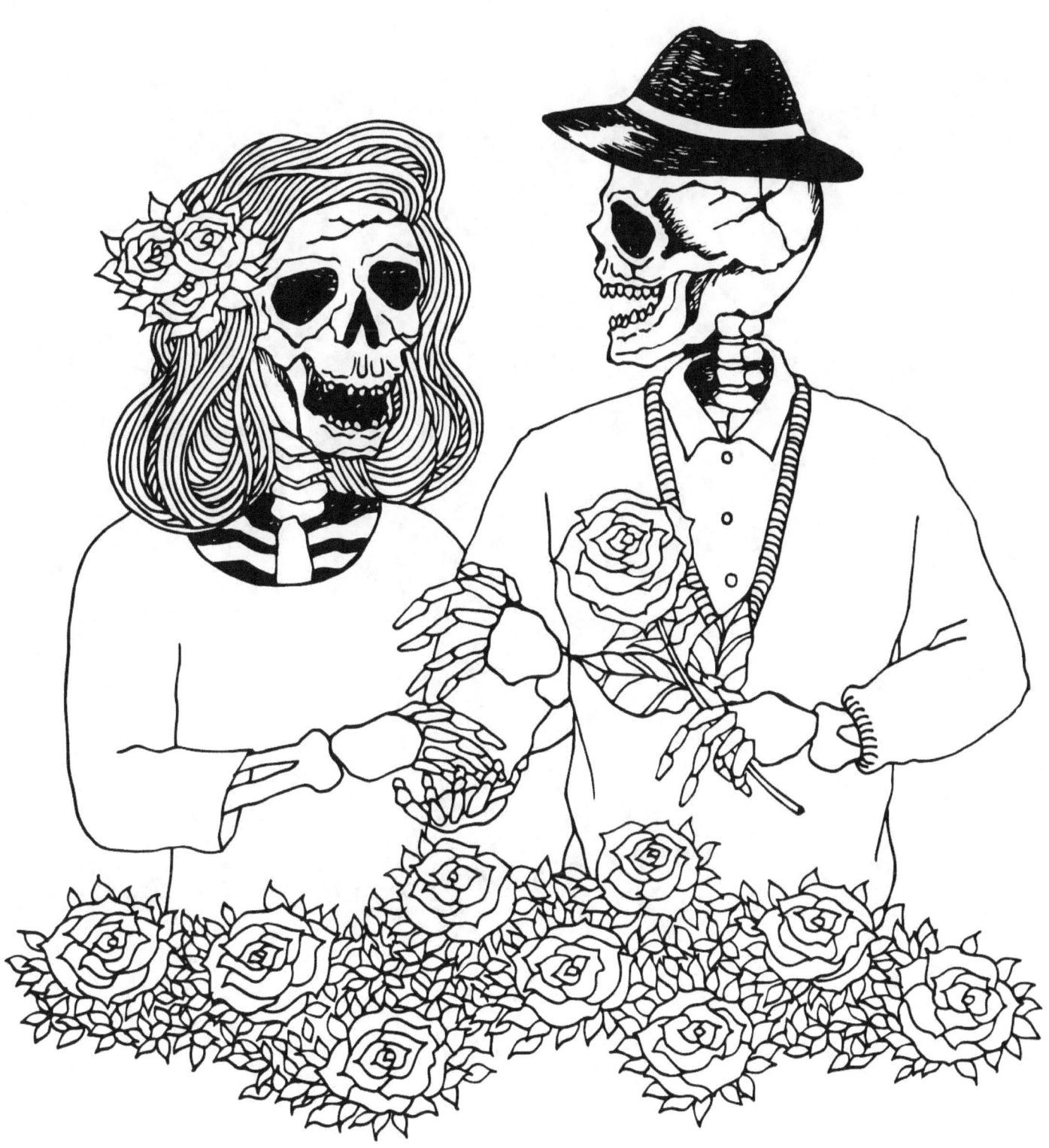

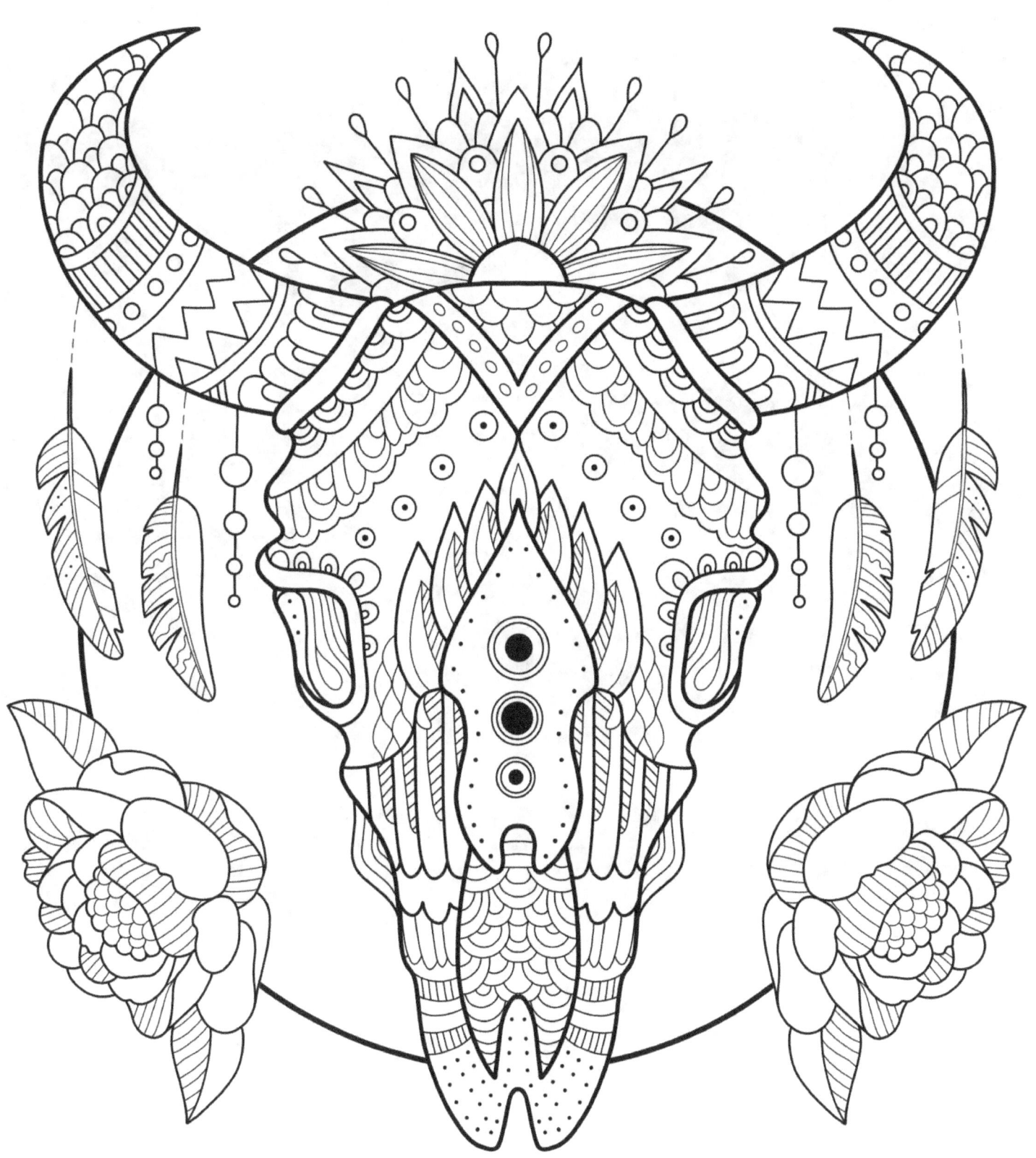

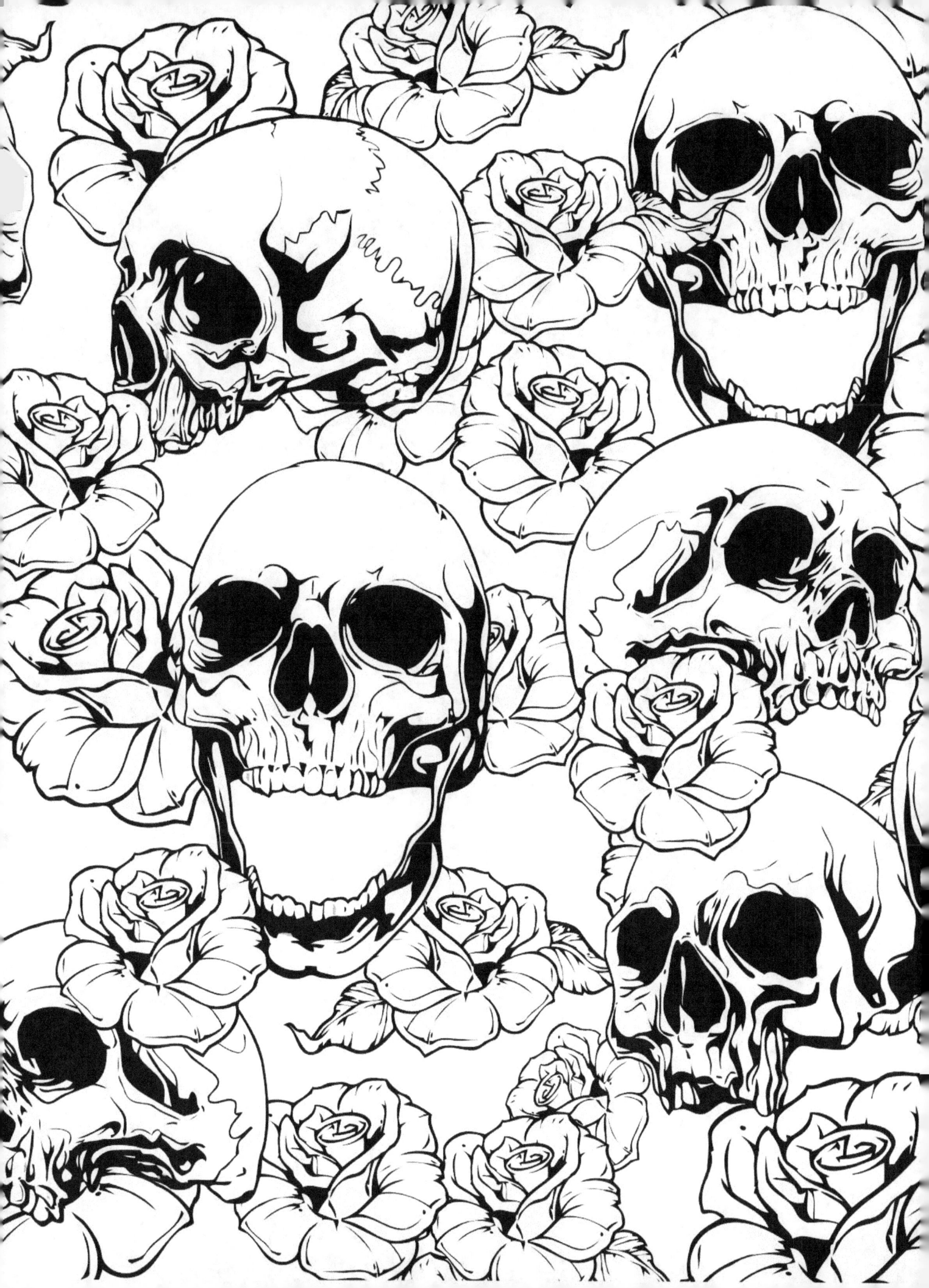

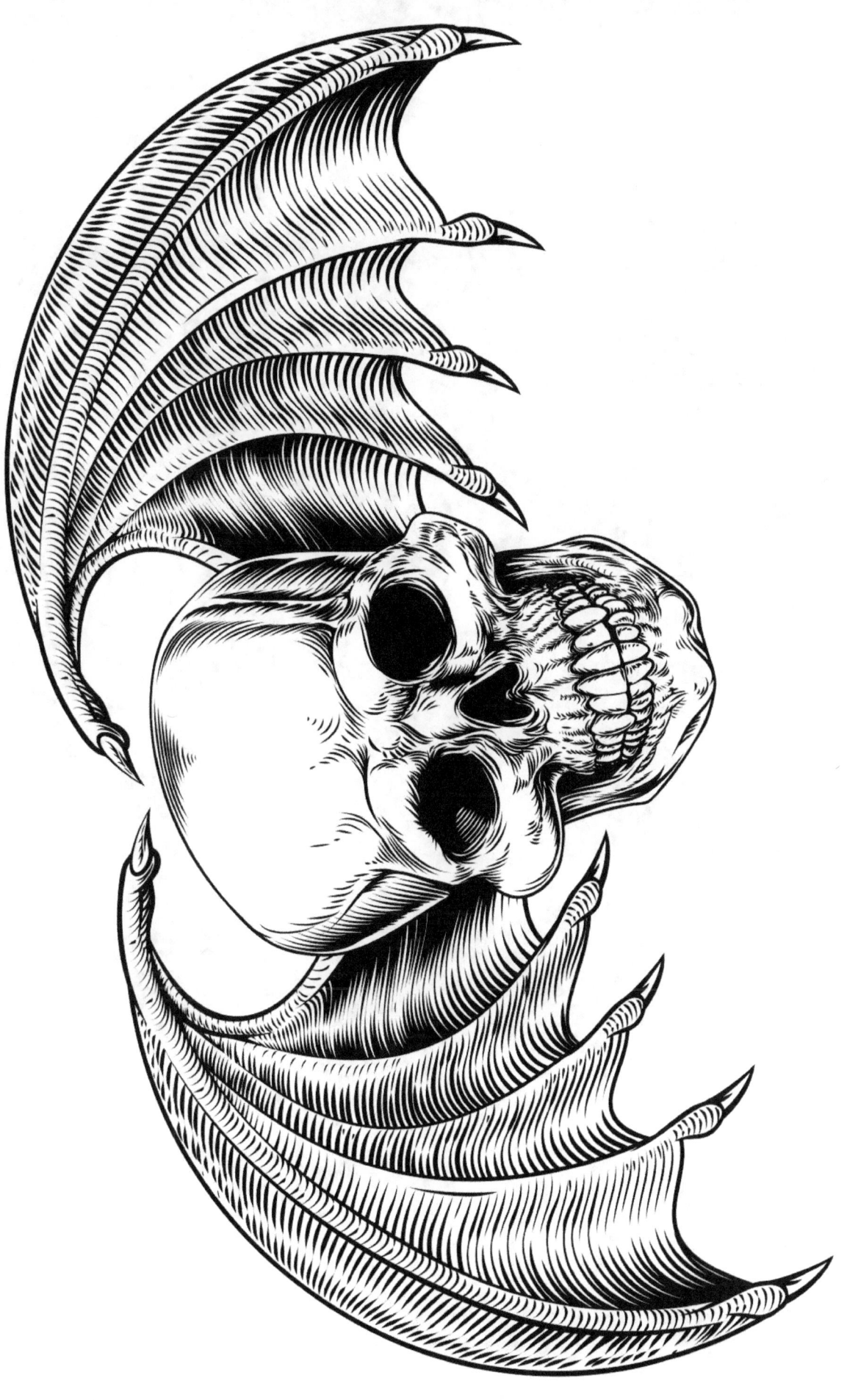

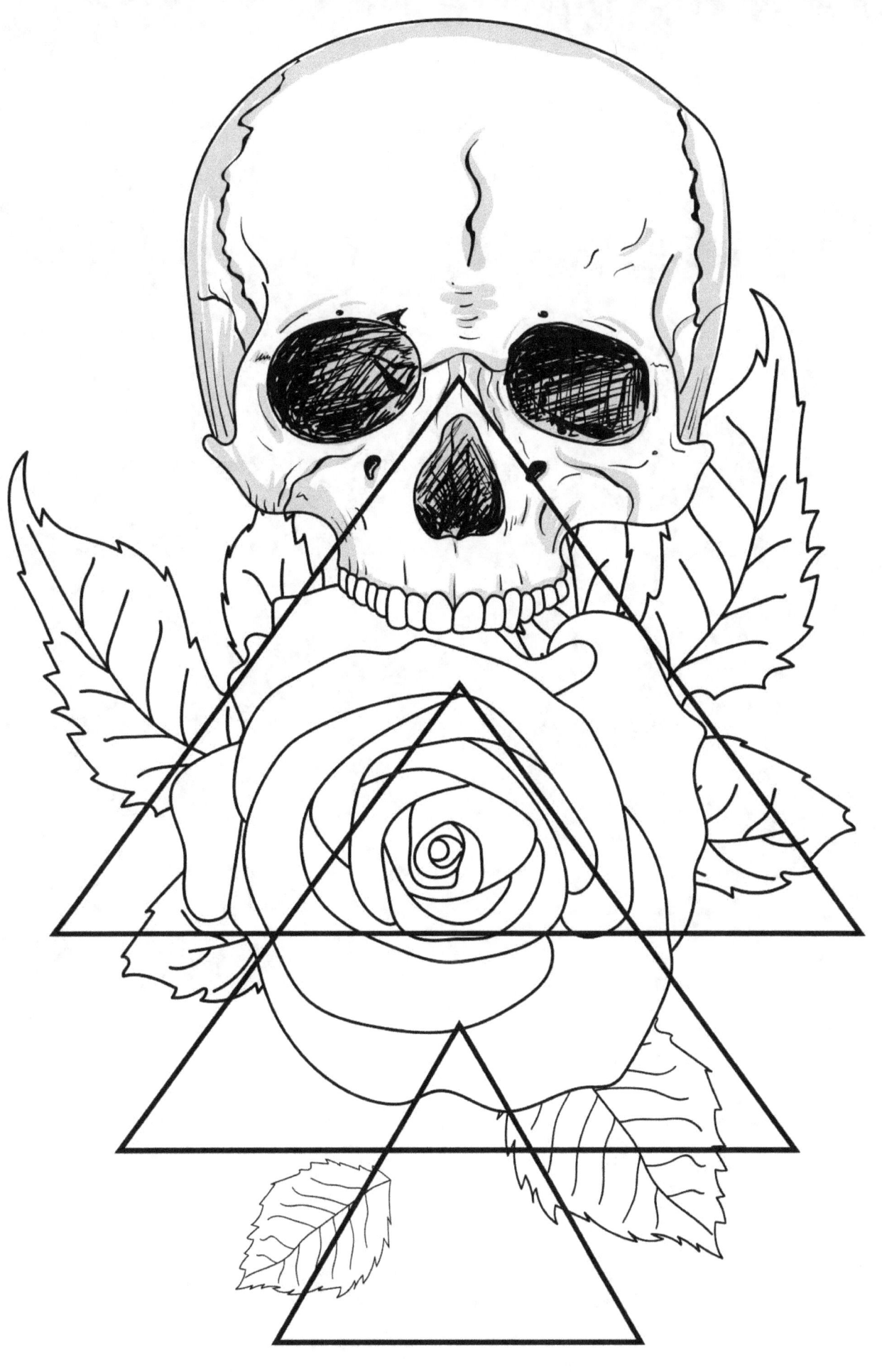

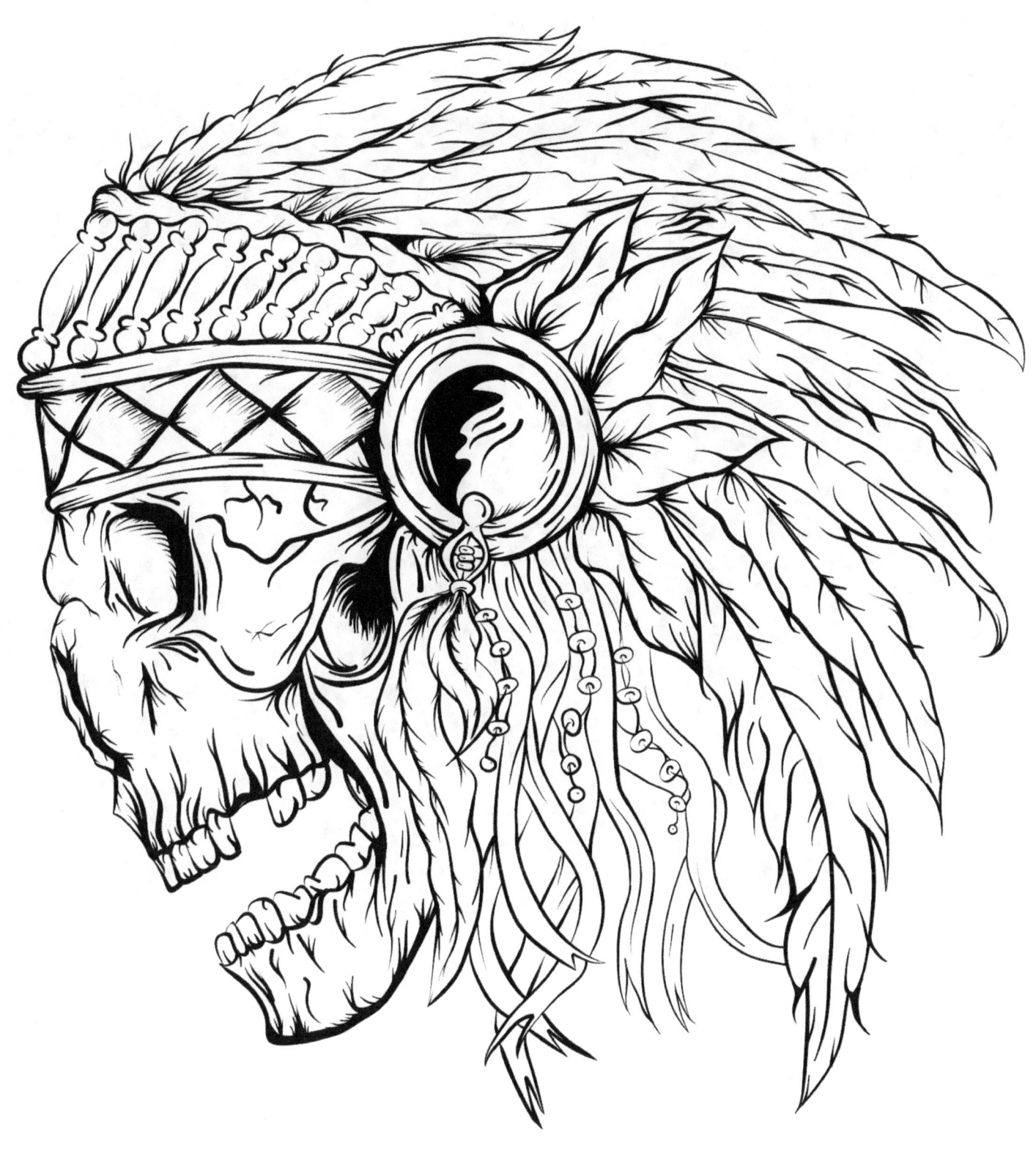

www.ingramcontent.com/pod-product-compliance
Lightning Source LLC
Chambersburg PA
CBHW081902170526
45167CB00007B/3120